P9-CNI-965

20TH CENTURY · DESIGN

40s AND 50s

WAR AND POST-WAR YEARS

20TH CENTURY DESIGN – '40s and '50s
was produced by

David West ♟ Children's Books
7 Princeton Court
55 Felsham Road
London SW15 1AZ

Picture research: Brooks Krikler Research
Editor: Clare Oliver
Additional research: Nesta Fitzgerald

First published in Great Britain in 1999 by
Heinemann Library, Halley Court, Jordan Hill,
Oxford OX2 8EJ, a division of Reed Educational and
Professional Publishing Limited.

OXFORD MELBOURNE AUCKLAND
JOHANNESBURG BLANTYRE GABORONE
IBADAN PORTSMOUTH (NH) USA CHICAGO

03 02 01 00 99
10 9 8 7 6 5 4 3 2 1

ISBN 0 431 03954 2 (HB)
ISBN 0 431 03955 0 (PB)

British Library Cataloguing in Publication Data

Jones, Helen
War and post-war (1940s - 1950s). - (Design in the
twentieth century)
1. Design - History - 20th century - Juvenile literature
I. Title
745.4'442

Printed and bound in Italy

*The dates in brackets after a designer's
name give the years that he or she lived.
Where a date appears after an object (or, in
the case of a building, the town where it is
situated), it is the year of its design.
'C.' stands for circa, meaning about or
approximately.*

*An explanation of difficult words can be
found in the glossary on page 30.*

20TH CENTURY · DESIGN

40s AND 50s

WAR AND POST-WAR YEARS

Helen Jones

Heinemann
LIBRARY

CONTENTS

During the war, people were encouraged to 'make do and mend', so as not to waste scarce resources.

One of the greatest technological milestones of the century came in '59, when the USSR launched the first satellite, Sputnik 1. The space age had begun.

WAR & PEACE

The 1940s began with a terrible war in Europe. Every resource was directed to the war effort, with the result that many new technologies developed.

Desperate shortages continued into peacetime and, for a while, so did the austere designs. Gradually economies recovered. Mass production enabled goods to be produced in large quantities at low prices and the consumer revolution began.

By the 1950s there was a general feeling of optimism. New buildings sprang up. Teenagers wore the latest fashions and bopped to the newest sounds.

Wartime bombing had reduced many of Europe's architectural landmarks to rubble. Post-war rebuilding was a major project with thousands of bombed homes to be replaced.

Families began to own television sets. With the advent of jetliners, foreign travel increased. Car ownership grew so dramatically that planners redesigned roads and cities.

Pop stars like Elvis Presley influenced how the teenagers spent their money and especially what they wore.

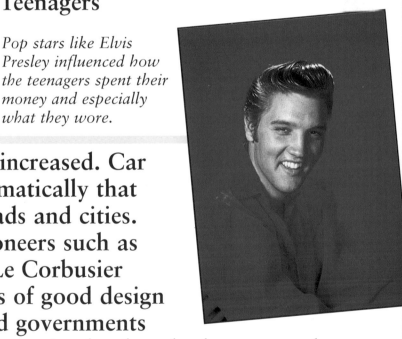

At the same time, pioneers such as Raymond Loewy and Le Corbusier promoted the principles of good design until manufacturers and governments understood its importance. As the decade drew to a close, consumers became ever more sophisticated. Designs were no longer only functional: they were futuristic or even downright wacky.

During the '50s, American cars featured exaggerated 'fins' as seen on this Chevrolet Impala ('59).

NFORMATION GRAPHICS

The war saw graphic designers, illustrators and artists using their skills to put across information or propaganda. Later, the same techniques were used to promote products and companies instead of countries.

The Utility logo ('42) used simple shapes to present the functional range of goods in a visual way.

POSTER POWER

During the war posters urged people to join the army or gave instructions, such as how to wear a gas mask. Others were propaganda, intended to instill in people patriotic hatred of the enemy. In Britain the official poster artist was Abram Games (1914–96). He favoured memorable sayings and produced the famous 'Careless Talk Costs Lives' posters.

POST-WAR POSTER POWER

After the war, designers continued to use symbols to represent ideas in a punchy way. For example, the Festival of Britain logo ('51), featuring the Union Jack colours and head of Britannia, was carefully designed to inspire pride in the nation.

Abram Games' logo for the Festival of Britain ('51) showed a stylised Britannia on a semicircle of red, white and blue flags.

FATHER OF DESIGN

Working in the US, French-born designer Raymond Loewy (1893–1986) pioneered good design. He recognised that consumers would grow more sophisticated. He advised manufacturers to woo their custom with elegant, streamlined designs. To their delight, they found the strategy worked.

In '49 Loewy became the first designer to appear on the cover of Time magazine. The caption read 'he streamlines the sales curve'.

DESIGNER RAYMOND LOEWY
He streamlines the sales curve.

Swiss-born typographer Adrian Frutiger designed the Univers typeface in '54. Univers was an instant success. Its simple lines made it appear ultra modern. It was one of the first sans serif faces.

ABCDEFGHIJKL UVWXYZ a

6

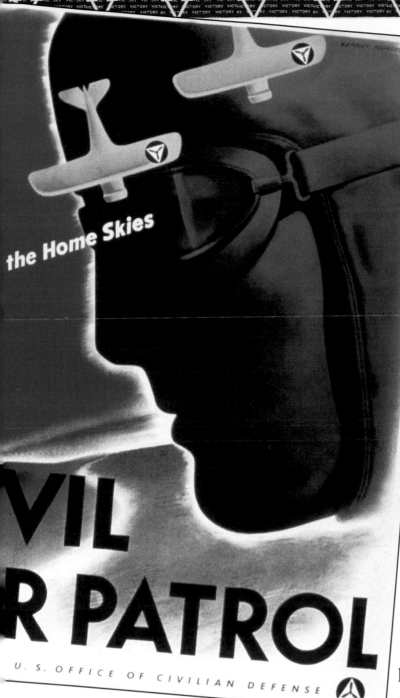

the Home Skies

VIL
R PATROL

U. S. OFFICE OF CIVILIAN DEFENSE

This poster, produced by the US government in '43, was intended to reassure people of their safety. It uses sans serif type (so its name is easy-to-read) and cheery, patriotic colours.

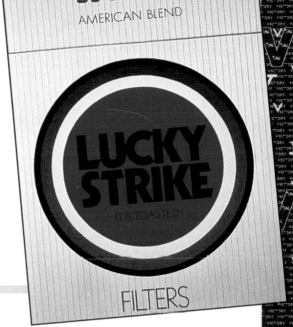

Loewy's redesign of the Lucky Strike cigarette packet (1940–2), with its bold sans serif type and eye-catching 'bullseye' background, has remained unchanged for 60 years.

LONG-TERM LOGOS

As companies became more aware of the power of branding, they commissioned top designers to create logos to last a lifetime. They hoped to attract loyal customers who would stick to one brand that they recognised. Paul Rand's logo for IBM (1956) was one of the most successful, long-lasting symbols of corporate identity. Rand's clarity of design stemmed from his ability to break the logo down into simple, timeless shapes.

Loewy's logos also used basic shapes. His timeless designs are still recognisable today.

SIMPLE TEXT

These words you are reading now are printed in a serif typeface, with decorative strokes on the letters. In the 1940s and '50s, typographers felt that the clean lines of typefaces that were sans (without) serif, such as Univers, were more modern.

cdefghijklmnopqrstuvwxyz 1234567890

DESIGN & TECHNOLOGY AT WAR

DFaced with the urgent demands of war, scientists and engineers came up with wonder medicines and new materials. Brand new technologies, such as nuclear power and computers, were developed. Some of the greatest advances were in aviation.

Curtiss planes were some of the first to be built entirely from stressed metal. The paintwork harks back to the decorative habits of ancient warriors.

8

Attacking from altitudes of over 7,600 m, at speeds of 300 km/h, Boeing's B-17 Fortress could drop 1,800 kg of bombs. Even these mighty fighting machines bore painted mascot figures.

HIGH FLYERS

Military planes developed rapidly. Producing ever-faster fighters, bombers and spy planes, nations battled for air supremacy. But engineers were hampered by limited resources. The American fighter plane Kittyhawk (1942), for example, did not fly as fast as it might. The turbo-superchargers it needed to boost its engine were scarce, and were allocated to bombers instead. Even so, Kittyhawk's engine was 20 times more powerful than the engine of a modern family car!

ROCKET SCIENTISTS

On 3 October 1942, the Germans successfully launched their A-4 long-range bombardment missile, known to the Allies as the V2, or Vengeance Weapon 2. It was the first ever space rocket and successfully hit its target 192 kilometres away.

COMPUTER AGE

Colossus, completed in '43, was an early British-built computer. As long as four buses, it was used to decipher codes created by the German machine, Enigma. After the war, scientist John von Neumann, working in the USA, suggested using binary code to store information. This allowed computers to get smaller!

US computer for building missiles ('50).

A V2 rocket was launched in New Mexico, October '46. After the war, German engineers went to the USA with enough material to make 100 V2s.

The V2's motor ran on alcohol and liquid oxygen. After about a minute, the rocket reached its target speed of 5,500 km/h and the motor cut out. The rocket continued to its target in freefall. The Germans built over 6,000 V2s and after the war its engineers were tempted to the United States and to the USSR. This amazing missile was the forerunner of modern guided missiles and also of all rockets used in space launches.

DAWN OF THE NUCLEAR AGE

The US dropped the first nuclear bombs on the Japanese cities of Hiroshima and Nagasaki in '45. Nuclear power was achieved by splitting the nucleus, or centre, of an atom of a heavy element, such as plutonium or uranium. This splitting, called nuclear fission, produces a sudden burst of enormous energy. The uranium bomb dropped on Hiroshima flattened an area of ten square kilometres.

9

Models of Little Boy and Fat Man, the bombs dropped on Hiroshima and Nagasaki in '45.

The US carried out more nuclear experiments after the war, with tests near the Bikini Atoll in the Pacific in '54.

Nuclear power was also developed to drive submarines and to provide a renewable source of energy for homes. The first commercial nuclear power plant opened in the UK in '56 at Calder Hall.

Atomic test at the Bikini Atoll ('54).

ON THE ROAD

During the war, petrol was in short supply and in Britain petrol remained rationed until 1954. For most people, this made the car an unaffordable luxury.

INDIVIDUAL FREEDOM

During the 1950s, as average incomes rose and fuel supplies became more certain, more people in Europe and the United States bought cars. For Americans in particular, the freedom of the open road came to symbolise all sorts of dreams and aspirations. Car manufacturers such as Chrysler, Ford and Cadillac created futuristic designs that reflected this feeling of excitement and optimism.

10

Pointy metal tail fins typified the showy styling of the big American saloons, as seen on this Chevrolet Bel Air ('57).

Convertible cars, such as the Studebaker ('50) designed by Raymond Loewy, were a symbol of youth and glamour.

SHOWING OFF

A key look was exaggerated styling. Shiny chrome fins suggested speed. So too did a car that was higher at the front than at the back. The car's face-like quality – two headlamps for its eyes, a grille for the nose and fender for the mouth – was often emphasised. This made the vehicle seem like a loyal friend, endowed with a personality of its own.

The Messerschmitt Cabin Scooter ('56) was one of many European attempts at a miniature town car. It was cheap, but not very versatile.

SMALL IS BEAUTIFUL

While American cars grew bigger, the Europeans sought more economical forms of private transport. British, French and German designers developed new bubble cars, tricycles and motorcycles. These vehicles were very fuel efficient and were perfect for nipping about in cities.

SCOOTING ABOUT

Motor scooters were a perfect solution to war-torn economies as they used very little petrol. The Italian firm Piaggio brought out the Vespa in 1946. It stayed in production for over 40 years. It was successful because it was cheap to run, easy to drive and elegant to look at. Its fiercest competitor, the Lambretta, came out in '47. Each was aimed at both men and women.

PUBLIC TRANSPORT

Of course, not everyone had their own private form of transport. Buses and trams were still popular forms of public transport, and they did not escape restyling. Raymond Loewy worked on America's famous Greyhound buses in the 1940s. The coast-to-coast buses became a post-war design icon.

Loewy's redesigns for the Greyhound Bus Company gave the coaches a recognisable identity. They were curvy and streamlined.

Though its top speed was under 50 km/h, the Vespa was ideal for getting about the quiet '50s roads of the town or city.

THE GODDESS

In '55, the Citroën DS stunned the motoring world with its many futuristic features and streamlined styling. Where earlier cars relied on springs to cushion a bumpy ride, the DS used a radical system of water pressure to lift the car off the road, called hydropneumatic suspension. Even the car's rear window had been specially angled, so it would not need a windscreen wiper! And its aerodynamic body allowed it to take corners at high speed without tipping.

The Citroën DS (short for déesse, or 'goddess') was unveiled at the Paris Motor Show in '55.

TRANSPORT: FUTURE CONCEPTS

With the war behind them, designers looked to the future with optimism. Anticipating the space age, they produced prototypes for the transport of the future. Few of these were produced, but they inspired and influenced later designs.

Ford built this futuristic prototype ('54) from pearlised blue and red plastic.

SELF-DRIVING CARS

Everyone could see that the private car would become increasingly important as a form of travel. The American industrial designer Norman Bel Geddes (1893–1958) even suggested that in the city of the future, cars would be able to drive themselves along colour-coded roads! At the end of the 20th century, this looked set to become reality, with satellites (rather than coloured markings) controlling the cars.

TUCKER'S LUCK

In '48, American Preston Tucker founded a new car company to sell his revolutionary car, the 'Tin Goose'. Its styling was unique – features included swappable rear and front seats to minimise wear and tear. Technologically, too, the car was ahead of its time. For example, it was the first to use a self-contained water cooling system to regulate the temperature of the engine. Sadly, the company could not compete with the big-name brands. Only 51 Tuckers were built, of which 48 are still around today.

Tucker's 'Tin Goose' really flew! It could go from 0 km/h to 100 km/h in ten seconds and its top speed was almost 200 km/h.

Design for a prototype seaplane ('44) that would be able to carry 100 passengers and hit speeds of 550 km/h.

This prototype diesel train ('47) featured split-level seating. Its 'astrodome' roof gave passengers a perfect view.

The Routemaster was fuel-efficient and more stable than previous buses. It carried more passengers and used less fuel.

SEAPLANES

Designers around the world were also busy planning the new 'superliners' of the skies. Many were designed to use the sea as a giant runway, but this idea never really took off.

CHOO! CHOO!

Train transport was slow to adapt to new technologies, because the existing machinery was so expensive to replace. Steam engines remained a common sight on the railways of Europe and the United States into the 1960s. *Big Boy* was the largest and most powerful steam locomotive ever built. Although only 25 were produced (1941–4), they stayed in service for nearly 20 years before being replaced by the new diesel locomotives.

SPRUCE GOOSE

On 2 November '47 history was made when the Hughes H-4 Hercules seaplane made her maiden flight. The eight-engine machine, nicknamed the *Spruce Goose*, was made of plastic-impregnated wood. It was designed to carry 750 passengers but only ever made a single flight. Its designer Howard Hughes (1905–76) piloted it on the 1.6-km journey at Sacramento, California.

Howard Hughes' Spruce Goose ('47).

CLASSIC DESIGN

Some designs stayed on the drawing board for so long, that by the time they went into production they no longer seemed modern! The famous Routemaster double-decker bus was designed in 1954 by Douglas Scott (1913–90), but did not enter service until five years later, by which time critics complained it already looked old-fashioned. Even so, this classic design is still seen on London's streets.

THE JET AGE ARRIVES

The era of modern mass air travel began in earnest after World War II. By the end of the 1950s, jet planes were the most important means of international travel.

Sir Frank Whittle (right) demonstrates his jet engine to the press ('48).

The early jet fighter, Gloster Meteor, took to the skies in '44. Hot on its tail was the Messerschmitt Me 262.

FATHER OF THE JET

Englishman Frank Whittle (1907–96) had the idea for the jet engine in 1928 and built a prototype in '37. The first jet aircraft to fly, however, was built in Germany by Ernst Heinkel (1888–1958) in '39. Heinkel had gleaned information from Whittle's '30 patent application. The first jet fighters included Germany's Messerschmitt Me 262 and the British Gloster Meteor. A Whittle engine was sent to the United States in '41, where the fighter P-80 Shooting Star was developed.

De Havilland's Comet 4 had reinforced round windows. These replaced the fatally flawed square windows of the Comet 2, which caused the disappearance of two planes.

14

JET ENGINES

In the jet engine, air is sucked in by a compressor (a series of fan-shaped blades), where it is compressed. Then, it enters the combustion chamber, where it mixes with fuel and ignites to create an explosion of gas. This rushes over a turbine (which drives the compressor fans) and out of the back of the engine in a jet, powerfully thrusting the plane forward.

Turbine   *JET ENGINE*

Exhaust gases provide thrust

Combustion chamber

Air is sucked in and compressed

WHAT A DRAG

At the same time, designers came up with new ways to add lift at take-off and to slow the plane down when landing. Slats on the wings or adjustable flaps meant that the wings themselves could get smaller. This reduced the overall weight of the plane and made flying times quicker.

MAIDEN VOYAGE

On 3 May 1952, the BOAC (British Overseas Airways Corporation) opened the first commercial jet airliner service. The BOAC Comet, designed by British company de Havilland, flew from London to Johannesburg – nearly 11,000 kilometres – in under 24 hours, cutting the previous flight-time by half.

The first Boeing 707 rolls off the assembly line ('57). At over 30 m long and weighing in at 112,500 kg, it was the largest jetliner ever built.

CLASSIC PLANE

The classic Boeing 707 made its first flight on 20 December 1957. It marked the first serious competition for the Comet and the beginning of the end for the great ocean liners such as the *Queen Mary*. Like the *Queen Mary*, the 707 could carry about 180 passengers across the Atlantic, but the ship cost six times more to build, guzzled ten times as much fuel and was a lot slower. The jet age had arrived at last.

THE KOREAN WAR

The World War II jet fighter appeared too late to have any serious impact. The first real jet combat was the Korean War (1950–3). American-built F-86 Sabres were pitted against Soviet MiG-15s. Both had swept-back wings to reduce drag. They had top speeds of well over 1,100 km/h and could break the sound barrier in a dive.

Although the MiG-15 flew faster, the F-86 was more controllable and proved more successful.

LIVING SPACES

During the war, millions of buildings were destroyed by air raids. At the same time, few new ones were built because resources were scarce. Once the war was over, serious rebuilding began.

Bomb damage destroyed many terraced homes (right, '41), and architects took up the challenge to replace them (below, '48).

BRITISH SPIRIT

Architecture lifted people's spirits after the war. Built for the Festival of Britain (1951), the Royal Festival Hall by Leslie Martin (*b*.1908) and Peter Moro (*b*.1911) attracted over eight million visitors. Its modernist style owed much to Le Corbusier, with classical proportions and modern details. Also featured were the temporary space-age Skylon by Philip Powell (*b*.1921) and Hidalgo Moya (1920–94) and the Dome of Discovery by Ralph Tubbs (1912–96).

16

Inside the Dome of Discovery, the latest inventions were on display. At the time, it was the largest dome in the world.

HOMES FOR HEROES

Architecture also had a more urgent task. Promises of 'Homes for Heroes' needed to be met. The solution was to apply the principles of the assembly line to architecture.

CONCRETE KING

Le Corbusier (1887–1965) believed in pre-fabricated, mass-produced high-rise homes. Inspired by machines, ships and aeroplanes as well as by classical architecture, his concept of the home as a 'machine for living in' was realised in the housing scheme he built in Marseilles, France, called *Unité d'Habitation* (1946–52).

BRUTAL BEAUTY

The expressive use of concrete in bold forms was dubbed brutalism. The International Style of architecture stripped down buildings to their basic elements, usually concrete structures and glass facades or skin. Reinforced concrete now allowed architects to build structures in which the walls were non-loadbearing. By composing buildings as simple units of concrete and glass, architects were able to build quickly, using prefabricated elements. Architects such as Richard Neutra (1892–1970) in California, and Peter Womersley in Britain, placed their buildings carefully in the landscape and then used glass to blur the barriers between interior and exterior space, bringing the outside inside.

Farnley Hey, Yorkshire ('55), designed by Peter Womersley, has many large windows which draw the landscape into the living space.

With his Chapel of Notre Dame-du-haut ('55), Le Corbusier showed off concrete's versatility. It could be set into sculptural shapes: this church was inspired by a shell!

Le Corbusier's Unité d'Habitation in Marseilles is the perfect 'machine for living in'. Raised off the ground on concrete pilotis, it contains over 300 chic apartments, all with double-storey living rooms, plus shops, a gym and a rooftop swimming pool!

SET IN CONCRETE

Concrete was the perfect building material for the modernist architects: they could mould it into any shape, and create buildings like sculptures. It was also cheap, consisting of water, cement and aggregate (a mixture of sand and gravel). To give it extra strength, it was reinforced with steel rods. This technique had developed in France a century earlier, using iron rods.

A network of steel rods are placed in the form or mould

Liquid concrete is poured in

The form is removed, leaving hardened, reinforced concrete

BUILD IT BIG

The International Style became the architectural symbol for the post-war age, especially in the United States. Working in steel, concrete and glass, architects created gleaming glass towers and organic concrete creations.

The first McDonalds ('55) had instantly-recognisable, curved concrete arches. The company knew the power of branding.

18

NEW YORK GIANT

Soaring skyscrapers were a form of status symbol. In the competitive post-war years, companies had to develop their image or brand. The most stunning skyscraper of all, the 38-storey Seagram Building (1955–8) was built by Ludwig Mies van der Rohe (1886–1969). A model of uncompromising beauty, it is made of glass and bronze-covered steel. Originally the inside bore murals by artist Mark Rothko (1903–70) which provided more abstract rectangles.

CURVY CONSTRUCT

Designers unveiled this vision of the petrol station of the future in '44. They correctly anticipated the use of pre-fab concrete in curvy, organic shapes. But while service stations at the end of the 20th century did have stream-lined pumps and restaurants, none had a heliport on its roof!

Futuristic design for a petrol station.

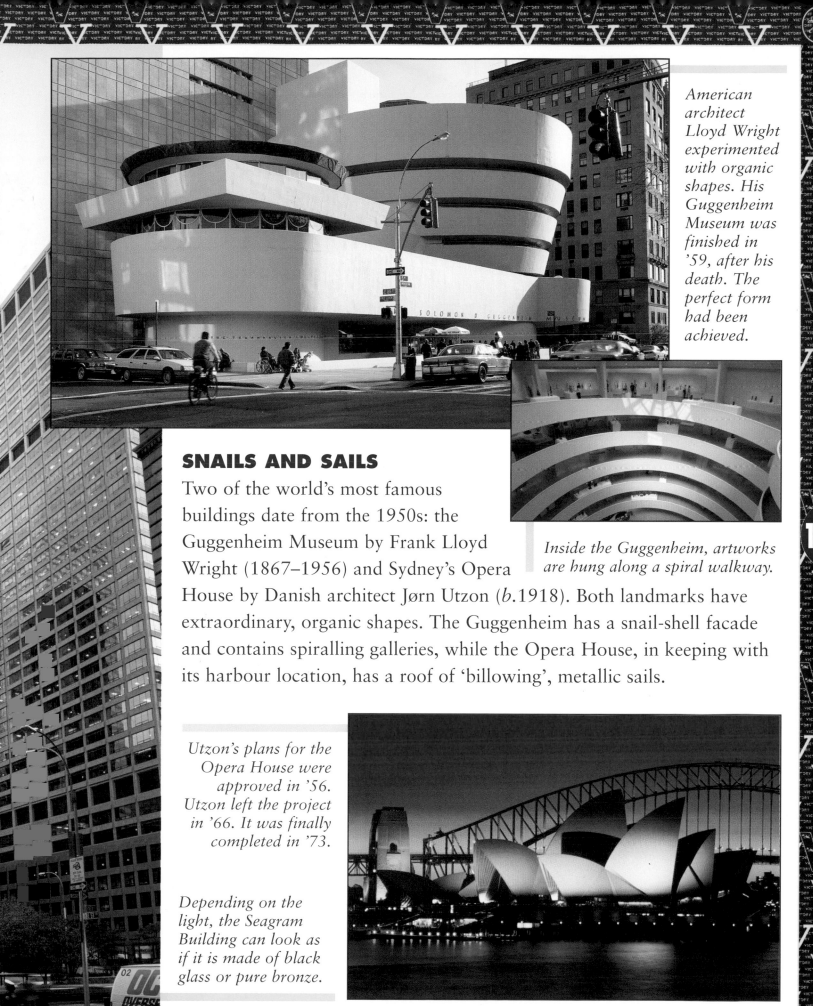

American architect Lloyd Wright experimented with organic shapes. His Guggenheim Museum was finished in '59, after his death. The perfect form had been achieved.

Inside the Guggenheim, artworks are hung along a spiral walkway.

SNAILS AND SAILS

Two of the world's most famous buildings date from the 1950s: the Guggenheim Museum by Frank Lloyd Wright (1867–1956) and Sydney's Opera House by Danish architect Jørn Utzon (*b*.1918). Both landmarks have extraordinary, organic shapes. The Guggenheim has a snail-shell facade and contains spiralling galleries, while the Opera House, in keeping with its harbour location, has a roof of 'billowing', metallic sails.

Utzon's plans for the Opera House were approved in '56. Utzon left the project in '66. It was finally completed in '73.

Depending on the light, the Seagram Building can look as if it is made of black glass or pure bronze.

INTERIORS

During the war, people had more pressing concerns than decor. Interiors remained in the muted greens and browns of the 1930s. After the war, interest in interiors returned.

INSPIRATION FROM ART

Bold, geometric designs replaced gloomy florals. The work of Paul Klee (1879–1940) created a vogue for patterns of coloured squares on sofas and chairs. The squiggly creations of Joan Miró (1893–1983) were copied on carpets, curtains and ceramics. And the 'drip and splash' style of Jackson Pollock's (1912–56) paintings appeared on wallpapers and textiles.

In an open-plan office ('53), information could be swapped freely. Doors were barriers between employees.

CONTEMPORARY STYLE

Just as architects tried to topple the division between inside and out, interior designers favoured airier, lighter buildings. They achieved this with open plan spaces. By the 1950s, traditional room divisions had been abandoned, in the home and the office.

FUTURE INTERIOR?

This display from '56 showed some of the features of the 'living space of the '80s'. At the touch of a button, the dining table rises from the floor. The dining chairs fold away when not in use. The designers correctly anticipated remote control TV, but the woman's hostess trolley, and the nylon clothes worn by the couple, are far more '50s than '80s!

A '50s vision of the interior of the future.

Designer Charles Eames and wife Ray in the living room of their California home. The airy, double-storey room had an extra feeling of space because the plants and huge windows brought the outdoors in.

Fitted kitchens took over from freestanding cupboards and cookers in the '50s.

KNOCKING THROUGH

Existing homes were also given the open-plan treatment. The wall dividing a living room and dining room was often knocked down, or replaced with a glass sliding door.

MAKING DO

For those who could not afford to completely transform their homes there was do-it-yourself (DIY). Couples used a range of new materials to modernise their homes and especially their kitchens. Formica gave old table tops a new lease of life. PVC blinds replaced curtains, wallpapers were wipe-clean and floors were covered with patterned linoleum (lino).

Split levels were used to define different living areas ('58).

21

Open-plan 'lounge-diners' became popular in the '50s.

FURNITURE

During wartime rationing and beyond, designers strove to create functional, affordable furniture.

FAIR FURNITURE

In Britain, the Board of Trade brought in the Utility furniture scheme in 1941. The scheme rationed how much was produced and limited available styles. Only those with a genuine need – newly-weds setting up home, for example, or families whose homes had been bombed – were allowed to buy it.

3-D MOULDING

During the war, new techniques for moulding plywood were discovered. American designer Charles Eames (1907–78) and his wife Ray (1916–88) spent the war years making stretchers and leg splints. They bent the plywood into shape by steaming it against a mould. They later used the same curved moulds for fibre glass and plastic.

An exhibition of Utility furniture ('42): fabrics came in sensible colours that would not show the dirt, while dining chairs were low-backed to save wood.

French designer Charlotte Perriand was influenced by Le Corbusier. This bookcase makes a colourful 'machine for storing books'.

AFFORDABLE FURNITURE

Plywood, fibre glass and plastic were all perfect materials for mass production. At last ordinary people could buy stylish, well-designed furniture. The first plastic chair off the production line was Charles Eames' Shell Chair. It was inexpensive, light, hard-wearing and easy to store.

The prototype of Arne Jacobsen's Ant Chair ('52) was made of moulded plywood. Later models came in bright colours.

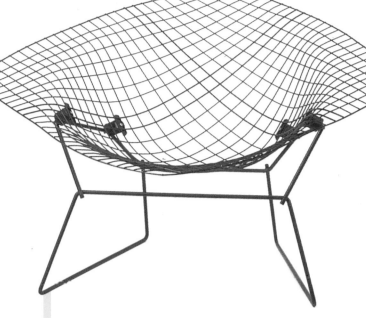

Movie star Stewart Granger's Hollywood home featured zebra bar stools with tubular steel legs. The television set was the ultimate luxury.

LEGS OF STEEL

Steel rods and steel wire were a

Despite the use of steel wire, Bertoia's Diamond Chair ('52) was expensive, because the metal had to be hand-welded.

popular choice for chair legs, including the famous three-legged Ant Chair designed by the Danish architect Arne Jacobsen (1902–71). But the Italian-born sculptor Harry Bertoia (1915–78) went one further. His Diamond Chair was made out of nothing but wire – and was the lightest, airiest chair ever seen!

FUNCTION AND FUN

American designer George Nelson (1908–86) was hugely influential. From '44 he directed the furniture company Herman Miller. There he created the Storage Wall, a divider for open-plan offices, along with flexible furniture systems: units that slotted together to create tailor-made storage. Nelson is probably best-remembered for a far less serious piece – his amazing Marshmallow Sofa. With squishy cushions in bright candy colours, this 3-D sculpture anticipated the pop art furniture of the next decade.

The Marshmallow Sofa ('56) was one of the first pieces of pop art furniture. George Nelson redesigned the traditional sofa, using marshmallow-shaped cushions with spaces between.

CLASSIC PRODUCTS

The demand for household goods and new electrical gadgets rose dramatically after the war. Manufacturers were using better plastics than ever before and designers were creating classics that have barely changed since.

Plastic Tupperware containers became popular in the '50s. Housewives sold them at Tupperware parties which they held for their friends.

THE STORY OF TUPPERWARE

During the 1930s, the American entrepreneur Earl Tupper had made a high-quality plastic that was durable, flexible and, most importantly, non-toxic and odourless. After using it for gas masks in the war, Tupper went on to make food storage boxes with a unique, airtight seal. This kept food moist in the dry air of the new refrigerators. His Tupperware was launched in '46.

Plastic-shelled transistor radios came in modern colours. Pastel pinks and lemon yellows were firm favourites.

24

INJECTION MOULDING

Hopper

Screw motor

Pellets of plastic

Final moulded plastic object

Heat

Molten plastic is forced into cool mould

Early plastics, such as Bakelite, were thermosetting plastics. This meant that they could not be reheated and reshaped once they had set. But after the war a new generation of plastics, called thermoplastics, were developed. These were more flexible than earlier plastics. They could also be injection moulded, which made them ideally suited for mass production.

In a screw injection moulding machine like this one, hard pellets of plastic are poured from a hopper on to a turning screw. Inside the screw, the pellets of plastic resin are heated and melt. When enough plastic has melted, the screw forces it into the cool mould. Inside, the plastic quickly solidifies, then the mould springs open, and the plastic part is pushed out by ejector pins.

Parts of a plastic doll, still in the mould ('51).

RADIO TIMES

Innovations after the war improved portable radios. Transistors and printed circuits replaced vacuum tubes and wires, so radios needed less power and could become smaller. Sound quality improved and FM stereo was introduced. Companies such as Pam and Sony competed for a share of the market with candy-coloured 'American-style' models in pastel plastics.

THE BRAUN RAZOR

The German electronic firm Braun had strong ideas about design – that it should be simple and uncluttered. This style was known as neofunctionalism. The company's best-known designer, Dieter Rams (*b.*1932), designed the electric razor in 1951. It had an oscillating motor in a simple case and ran on rechargeable batteries.

This electric razor for Braun was typical of neofunctional German styling. The basic design has hardly changed since.

SUCKING UP

Stockholm firm Electrolux asked Sixten Sason (1912–69) to create the perfect vacuum cleaner for them after World War II. The Swede's streamlined design still looks modern today.

The Electrolux vacuum cleaner ('54) had a bendy hose and various attachments which made it more flexible than heavy, rigid, upright models.

WHAT'S ON TELLY?

TV ownership increased rapidly. In '40 there were 10,000 televisions in the US; by '58, there were 50 million. Colour TVs came in at the beginning of the '50s. By the end of the decade, Japanese firm Sony had even produced a 'pocket' TV – its TV8-301 transistor television.

A family watch colour TV ('54).

DESIGN IN THE HOME

The myth of the perfect housewife-as-hostess was promoted during the 1950s, alongside the belief that beautifully-designed domestic appliances could turn housework into pleasure. According to the adverts, using these gadgets would give housewives more leisure time. In reality, while homes became far more hygienic, housework remained as time-consuming as ever.

TECHNOLOGY IN THE HOME

During the 1950s, many families installed telephones for the first time. Electricity had been installed in many homes during the '30s, but it was not until the post-war years that electrical appliances became common. For the first time housewives could use electric washing machines, vacuum cleaners, electric fires and kettles and soon the refrigerator would be here to stay. The electric home was fast becoming a reality.

CLASSIC KETTLE

Plug-in kettles replaced stove-top ones. The K2 kettle was designed in 1959 by WM Russell for Russell Hobbs. It was part of their 'Forgettable' range, so-called because the products had automatic cut-off switches. This was a huge improvement on previous electric kettles, which, when forgotten, would just keep boiling until the element burnt out.

The K2 could boil water in seconds and featured a cool-touch handle and lid knob. Most importantly, it switched itself off when the water had boiled.

THE FIRST MICROWAVE

Radar was developed during World War II and used invisible waves to detect enemy planes. Then scientist Percy Spencer noticed that the 'microwaves' had also melted the chocolate bar in his pocket. Raytheon's Radar Range, brought out in '47, was the first oven to use these microwaves. It caused a sensation when it cooked a burger in 35 seconds flat. But with a price tag of $3,000, it cost more than a family house!

CLEAN LINES

The United States led the way with the styling of the new domestic goods. Industrial designers such as Raymond Loewy applied the same streamlined look to refrigerators as they did to motor vehicles, producing a modern, curvy style. The common feature of all the latest designs was that they were sleek. The home had to be thoroughly hygienic and this was made easier as households purchased fitted kitchens, and wall-to-wall carpets.

In the '50s, homes grew brighter and sleeker. Kitchens were neat, fitted and spotlessly clean.

The Kenwood food mixer of the '40s, designed by Kenneth Grange, had attachments that still feature today. Early models also had a cutlery buffer for polishing silverware!

PAYING THE PRICE

The consumer revolution began in the United States. People were encouraged to buy more products after the introduction of hire purchase (HP), a kind of credit. Instead of paying at once, people could take their goods home and pay for them a little bit each week.

At the end of the 20th century, the fridge door 'aqua tap' came back into vogue. This clever chilled water dispenser first appeared in the '50s.

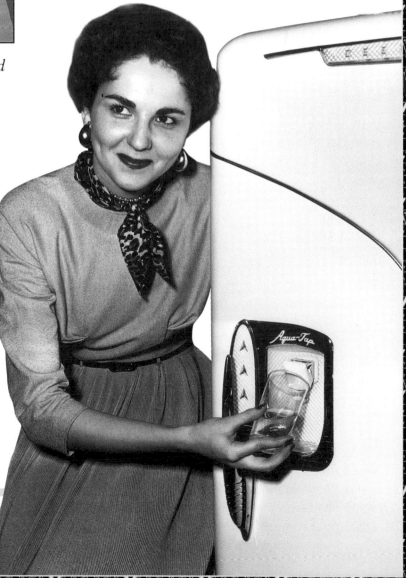

FASHION

The 1940s and '50s saw many changes in clothes design, especially in womenswear.

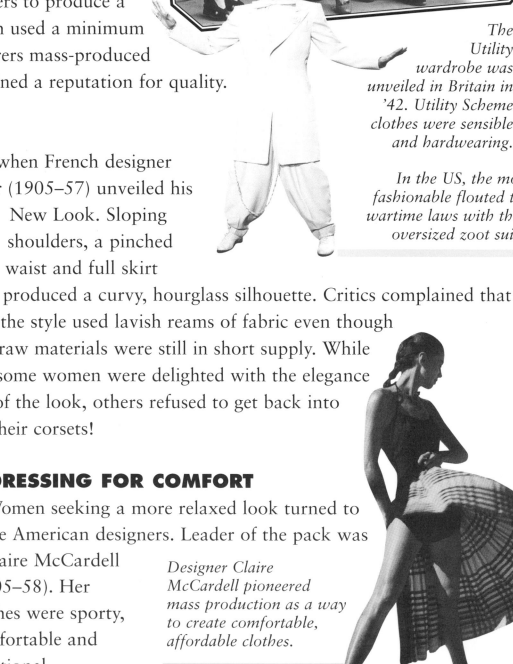

WARTIME AUSTERITY

In the United States, the L85 laws controlled the use of precious wool and silk. In Britain, the government asked top designers to produce a basic 'Utility' wardrobe which used a minimum of cloth. Licensed manufacturers mass-produced the clothes, which quickly gained a reputation for quality.

DIOR'S NEW LOOK

In 1947, femininity returned when French designer Christian Dior (1905–57) unveiled his New Look. Sloping shoulders, a pinched waist and full skirt produced a curvy, hourglass silhouette. Critics complained that the style used lavish reams of fabric even though raw materials were still in short supply. While some women were delighted with the elegance of the look, others refused to get back into their corsets!

The Utility wardrobe was unveiled in Britain in '42. Utility Scheme clothes were sensible and hardwearing.

In the US, the most fashionable flouted the wartime laws with their oversized zoot suits!

This Dior design of '47 shows the hourglass silhouette. The woollen coat opens to reveal a pleated taffeta skirt.

DRESSING FOR COMFORT

Women seeking a more relaxed look turned to the American designers. Leader of the pack was Claire McCardell (1905–58). Her clothes were sporty, comfortable and functional.

Designer Claire McCardell pioneered mass production as a way to create comfortable, affordable clothes.

28

McCardell worked in ordinary fabrics, such as cotton, jersey and denim. Most of the clothes were separates, including her wraparound skirt, designed to be mixed and matched.

The twinset – a matching knitted top and cardigan – was a popular '50s style. Here it is worn with a wraparound skirt.

THE RISE OF YOUTH CULTURE

The late 1950s saw the birth of the teenager, as the baby boomers (babies born just after the war) grew up. Novels and movies inspired them to develop their own styles: teenage tearaways wore jeans, teeshirts and leather jackets, while moody beatniks blurred the lines between male and female styles. These 'anti-fashions' were soon high fashion: in the '60s, youth styles came to dominate couture.

THE NYLON REVOLUTION

The fabric of the age was nylon, the first-ever synthetic fabric, which was patented by DuPont in '37. The first nylon stockings went on sale in the US in May '40 and sold out in four days. Nylon transformed the textile industry. It was easy to dye and the colour did not fade. It had a silky feel, but did not wrinkle or attract moths. Soon, it was being mixed with natural fibres and used for dresses, suits, ties and underwear as well as just stockings.

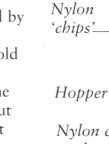

Nylon 'chips'

Hopper

Nylon chips are heated to make a viscous fluid

Cold air hardens the nylon thread

Nylon is forced through spinneret

Hot steam 'sets' or fixes the thread

Nylon filaments are twisted into yarn and rolled on to bobbin

French model Capucine teams beatnik pedal-pushers with a manly, outsize shirt ('58).

Nylon stockings are steamed into shape on metal moulds.

GLOSSARY

BRANDING A look for a product or company that consumers can recognise.

CONSUMER DURABLE A purchase that should last a long time, such as a kettle.

CONTEMPORARY STYLE Post-war style of furniture that aimed to be modern and affordable, as seen in the work of Charles Eames.

INJECTION MOULDING Technique for mass-producing thermoplastic products.

INTERNATIONAL STYLE Modernist designs with clean lines and no additional ornamentation. Examples are the Seagram Building and the Braun electric razor.

LOGO A symbol used to represent the name of a product or company in a recognisable, graphic way.

NEW LOOK At first, the name given to Dior's clothes collection in '47. Later, the term also referred to modern furniture and ceramics.

OPEN-PLAN Describes a style of interior where there are no walls. Space is divided by split levels, screens, or not at all.

ORGANIC Something that resembles a living thing from nature; often used to describe curvy shapes.

PILOTIS Pillars that support a building, raising it above the ground to second-storey level.

PRE-FAB Short for pre-fabricated. Describes buildings made of readymade modular units that were slotted together on site.

PROTOTYPE The original model of a product, from which the others are copied on the production line.

REINFORCED CONCRETE When steel rods are embedded into concrete before it sets in order to make it stronger.

SANS SERIF A typeface that does not have decorative serifs on the top and bottom of the letters.

STREAMLINING Aerodynamic design style featuring blunt, rounded edges, seen, for example, in the work of Loewy. Popular from the '30s to '50s.

TYPOGRAPHER A designer who selects or creates typefaces and decides how printed words should look.

30

DESIGN HIGHLIGHTS

• *Bel Geddes:* Magic Motorways	19
	19
• *Utility Scheme launched* • *Curtiss Kittyhawk*	19
	19
	19
	19
• *Vespa launched*	19
• *LEGO goes on sale* • *Dior: New Look*	19
• *Citroën 2CV launched* • *Tucker's 'Tin Goose'*	19
• *De Havilland: Comet* • *Loewy on cover of* Time	19
• *Loewy: Studebaker*	19
• *Festival of Britain*	19
• *Unité d'Habitation* • *Jacobsen: Ant Chair*	19
• *Chevrolet uses fibre-glass reinforcement*	19
• *Boeing 707* • *Univers typeface*	19
• *Citroën DS* • *Le Corbusier:* Notre Dame-du-Haut	19
• *IBM logo* • *Sydney Opera House designed*	19
	19
• *Seagram Building* • *Holtom: CND logo*	19
• *Austin Mini launched* • *Guggenheim completed*	19

TIMELINE

	WORLD EVENTS	TECHNOLOGY	FAMOUS PEOPLE	ART & MEDIA
40	•*World War II continues (1939–45)*	•*Nylon stockings go on sale*	•*Death of Paul Klee*	•*Stravinsky:* Symphony in C major
41	•*Japanese attack Pearl Harbor; USA enters war*	•*Big Boy locomotive built* •*Terylene invented*	•*Marriage of Charles & Ray Eames*	•*Brecht:* Mother Courage •*Coward:* Blithe Spirit
42	•*Oxfam founded*	•*Soft toilet paper introduced in Britain*	•*Gandhi imprisoned by British in India*	•*Bergman & Bogart star in Casablanca*
43	•*Mussolini arrested* •*Zoot suit riots in USA*	•*Colossus computer, UK*		•*Sartre:* Being and Nothingness
44	•*Allies land in France & drive back Germans*		•*Glenn Miller killed in plane crash*	•*Henry Moore:* Mother and Child
45	•*Germany & Japan surrender; war ends*	•*First atomic bombs* •*Microwave oven patented*	•*Suicide of Hitler* •*Truman becomes US President*	•*Britten:* Peter Grimes •*Steinbeck:* Cannery Row
46	•*UN General Assembly holds first meetings*	•*ENIAC computer built* •*Tupperware launched*		•*Picasso:* Reclining Nude •*O'Neill:* The Iceman Cometh
47	•*India & Pakistan gain independence*	•*Sound barrier broken by Yeager in US Bell X-1*	•*Howard Hughes pilots his Spruce Goose*	•*Cannes Film Festival opens* •*Camus:* The Plague
48	•*S. Africa: apartheid begins* •*Israel proclaimed*	•*Michelin: radial tyre* •*Transistor invented*	•*Gandhi assassinated*	•*Huston:* Key Largo •*John Wayne in* Red River
49	•*NATO set up* •*East & West Germany formed*		•*Mao proclaims Chinese People's Republic*	•*Orwell:* 1984
50	•*Korean War begins* •*China invades Tibet*	•*Gas turbine car (Rover)*	•*McCarthyism begins in USA*	•*Miró: mural for Harvard* •*Pollock:* Autumn Rhythm
51		•*First video recording* •*Braun electric razor*		•The African Queen
52	•*Kenya: Mau Mau revolt begins*		•*Elizabeth II proclaimed Queen of Britain*	
53	•*Korean War ends* •*Egypt: Nasser in power*	•*Crick & Watson describe DNA structure*	•*Norgay & Hillary climb Mt Everest*	•*Osborne:* Look Back in Anger •*Miller:* The Crucible
54	•*SEATO formed*	•*Trials of contraceptive pill* •*Atomic tests at Bikini Atoll*	•*Roger Bannister runs four-minute mile*	•*Kingsley Amis:* Lucky Jim •*Brando in* The Wild One
55	•*Warsaw Pact formed* •*S. Africa leaves UN*	•*Hovercraft patented* •*Optical fibres patented*	•*Einstein dies* •*Death of Jackson Pollock*	•*Patrick White:* Tree of Man •*Hitchcock:* Rear Window
56	•*Suez Crisis in Middle East*	•*First commercial nuclear power station opens, UK*	•*Elvis Presley's* Heartbreak Hotel *tops US record chart*	•*Allen Ginsberg:* Howl •*Beckett:* Waiting for Godot
57	•*EEC (Common Market) founded*	•*USSR launches first satellite, Sputnik 1*	•*Macmillan succeeds Eden as British prime minister*	•*Kerouac:* On the Road •*Chagall: The Circus Rider*
58	•*CND start anti-bomb protests*	•*Heart pacemaker invented*	•*De Gaulle elected president of France*	•*Chevalier & Caron star in* Gigi
59	•*Cuba: Castro in power* •*US troops sent to Laos*	•*Silicon chips first made* •*DuPont: Lycra*	•*Buddy Holly killed in plane crash*	

INDEX

32